Wow! That's Inspiring

Copyright © 2005 by Ron Kaufman.
All rights reserved. The moral right of the author has been asserted.

Published by Ron Kaufman Pte Ltd. - 10 9 8 7 6 5 4 3 2 1

Lift Me Up! - Wow! That's Inspiring!
ISBN 981-05-2935-X - 136 pages.

1. Inspiration
2. Quotations
3. Self-Help
4. Ron Kaufman
5. Title

Cover and page layout by The Bonsey Design Partnership.
Cover illustrations by Ngu Hie Ling.
Set in Times and Arial fonts. Printed in Singapore.

Every effort has been made to credit the original author and make full acknowledgement of the source for each quotation in this text. However, if you know of any instance where the quotation or citation could be more accurate, please send a message to Ron@RonKaufman.com Any corrections will gladly be included in future editions. Thank you.

Below each attributed quotation are **quips, quotes and anecdotes in bold text**. These additional notes are by Ron Kaufman (1956 –), who should be cited as the author in all future works.

Ron Kaufman, Lift Me Up!, Pick Me Up!, UP Your Service!, and a balloon with the word 'UP' are registered trademarks of Ron Kaufman Pte Ltd.

All rights reserved. No part of this book may be reproduced, stored, archived or transmitted in any form by mechanical or electronic means including information storage and retrieval systems without permission in writing from the publisher, except for the quotation of brief passages in book reviews.

Additional copies of this book are available at discount for promotional events, contests, awards, and in-house training programs. For details and fast delivery, contact:

Ron Kaufman Pte Ltd
50 Bayshore Park #31-01
Aquamarine Tower
Singapore 469977

Tel: (+65) 6441-2760
Fax: (+65) 6444-8292
Ron@RonKaufman.com
www.RonKaufman.com

Contents

Making dreams come true	4
Becoming an achiever	43
Overcoming obstacles	35
Living life fully	107

Making dreams come true

If you can dream it, you can do it.

Walt Disney

Dreams come true; without that possibility, nature would not incite us to have them.

John Updike

Dream on!

What dreams has nature given you?

If you don't have a dream, how are you going to make a dream come true?

Oscar Hammerstein

Hold fast to dreams, for without them we are like birds with broken wings.

Chinese proverb

If you could dream anything at all, what would you dream?

In your darkest hours, dreams light up your life.

So many of our dreams at first seem impossible, then they seem improbable, and then, when we summon the will, they soon become inevitable.

Christopher Reeve

The future belongs to those who believe in the beauty of their dreams.

Eleanor Roosevelt

You, too, can be Superman or Superwoman.

The future belongs to you. Believe it!

Small dreams have no power to move the hearts of men.

Johann Wolfgang von Goethe

When your dreams tire, they go underground and out of kindness that's where they stay.

Libby Houston

To move mountains (and people) dream BIG!

Keep your dreams above the ground, vital and alive!

You are never given a wish without also being given the power to make it true. You may have to work for it, however.

Richard Bach

All successful people are big dreamers. They imagine what their future could be, ideal in every respect, and then they work every day toward their distant vision, goal or purpose.

Brian Tracy

Do the work.

Imagine yourself totally successful. Then work to make it happen.

Peak performers develop powerful mental images of the behavior that will lead to the desired results. They see in their mind's eye the result they want, and the actions leading to it.

Charles Garfield

By recording your dreams and goals on paper, you set in motion the process of becoming the person you most want to be. What you think about comes about.

Mark Victor Hansen

To win the race, you must first win it in your mind.

Put your future in good hands – your own.

Only those who risk going too far can possibly find out how far one can go.

T.S. Eliot

You have to remember that seventy percent of the horses running don't want to win. Horses are like people. Everybody doesn't have the aggressiveness or ambition to knock himself out to become a success.

Eddie Arcaro

How far can you go?

If you are going to run, run to win!

Make no little plans!
They have no magic to
stir men's blood.

Daniel Burnham

If you can imagine it,
you can achieve it. If
you can dream it, you
can become it.

William Ward

**Become president,
travel to space, win a
Nobel prize. What's
your biggest plan?**

**And if you can do it, you
will enjoy it!**

I had ambition not only to go farther than any person had ever been before, but as far as it was possible for a person to go.

James Cook

Without ambition one starts nothing. Without work one finishes nothing.

Ralph Waldo Emerson

How far can you stretch your ambition?

Have the ambition to finish your work.

Aim for the top. There is plenty of room there. There are so few at the top it is almost lonely.

Samuel Insull

But not quite. And the company is very good.

It is funny about life: if you refuse to accept anything but the very best you will very often get it.

W. Somerset Maugham

And when you get it, enjoy it!

The greatest amount of wasted time is the time not getting started.

Dawson Trotman

Start right now.

All glory comes from daring to begin.

Eugene Ware

Go for it!

Take the first step in faith. You don't have to see the whole staircase, just take the first step.

Martin Luther King, Jr.

You can't cross the sea by standing staring at the water. At some point you must throw yourself in.

Ron Kaufman

Put your first foot forward.

Dive in!

Magic is believing in yourself. If you can do that, you can make anything happen.

Foka Gomez

**Believe in yourself.
Presto!**

Only those who dare to fail greatly can ever achieve greatly.

Frank Lloyd Wright

Take the risk.

The world is full of abundance and opportunity, but far too many people come to the fountain of life with a sieve instead of a tank car, a teaspoon instead of a steam shovel. They expect little and as a result they get little.

Ben Sweetland

Bring a big bucket and fill it up!

Success is not the result of spontaneous combustion. You must set yourself on fire.

Reggie Leach

You have within you the spark, the tinder and the fuel.

Begin doing what you want to do now. We are not living in eternity. We have only this moment, sparkling like a star in our hand and melting like a snowflake.

Marie Ray

Don't be afraid to take a big step. You can't cross a chasm in two small jumps.

David Lloyd George

Don't let this moment melt away. Begin now.

Everyone has fears, but some take the big step anyway. Will you?

Ambition never comes to an end.

Yoshida Kenko

I want to put a ding in the universe.

Steve Jobs

Let your ambition drive you.

Now it's your turn. Ding!

Aim for the highest.

Andrew Carnegie

A soul without a high aim is like a ship without a rudder.

Eileen Caddy

Aiming high can be unsettling in the beginning but highly rewarding in the end.

Let your soul steer your ship.

If you would hit the mark, you must aim a little above it; every arrow that flies feels the attraction of earth.

Henry Wadsworth Longfellow

Lord, grant that I may always desire more than I can accomplish.

Michelangelo

**Aim low, end up lower.
Aim higher, end up high.**

Let your desire be fuel for the fire.

Ah, but a man's grasp should exceed his reach, else what's a Heaven for?

Robert Browning

The man who removes a mountain begins by carrying away small stones.

Chinese proverb

Grasping at straws? Reach for Heaven!

A huge task may seem insurmountable until you begin with a first small step.

It has always seemed to me that the most difficult part of building a bridge would be the start.

Robert Benchley

The distance is nothing; it's only the first step that is difficult.

Marquis du Deffand

To create a bridge you must imagine reaching the end from the very beginning.

Take the first step toward your dreams.

If you wish to reach the highest, begin at the lowest.

Publilius Syrus

You climb every ladder from the bottom.

To accomplish great things, we must not only act, but also dream; not only plan, but also believe.

Anatole France

Have faith. Take action.

Everything's in the mind. That's where it all starts. Knowing what you want is the first step toward getting it.

Mae West

What do you want?

Do, or do not.
There is no 'try'.

Yoda (in *Star Wars*)

**Will you or won't you?
Just 'trying' is lying.**

Follow your dreams, for as you dream you shall become.

Helen Keller

There are some people who live in a dream world, and there are some who face reality; and then there are those who turn one into the other.

Douglas Everett

Sweet dreams!

Realistic dreamer or dreaming realist? Which are you?

Cherish your visions and your dreams as they are the children of your soul; the blueprints of your ultimate achievements.

Napoleon Hill

Dreams get you into the future and add excitement to the present.

Robert Conklin

Let your soul create your dreams and visions.

Let the show begin!

The only place where your dream becomes impossible is in your own thinking.

Robert Schuller

All our dreams can come true, if we have the courage to pursue them.

Walt Disney

Make your mind a positive place for possibilities.

Walt Disney went bankrupt before he succeeded. His courage brought Mickey Mouse to life. What will your courage bring?

It takes courage to tell other people your dreams.

Erma Bombeck

The only place you'll find success before work is in the dictionary.

May Smith

Share your dreams. Share your courage.

Dreams are where you're going and work is how you get there.

There are no short cuts to any place worth going.

Warren Buffett

Keep away from people who try to belittle your ambitions. Small people always do that, but the really great make you feel that you, too, can become great.

Mark Twain

Summiteers reach the peak step by careful step.

You *are* fantastic!

Surround yourself only with people who are going to lift you higher.

Oprah Winfrey

Set your goals high and don't stop until you get there.

Bo Jackson

Balloonists, hang-gliders, mountain climbers and you. Optimists all!

Keep on climbing.

First say to yourself what you would be; and then do what you have to do.

Epictetus

A goal is a dream with a deadline.

Zig Ziglar

You gotta do what you gotta do. There is no way around it.

Mark your calendar – done by *when?*

Opportunities multiply
as they are seized.

Sun Tzu

Opportunity is missed
by most people because
it is dressed in overalls
and looks like work.

Thomas Edison

Grab the first one. Here comes another!

Get your blue jeans on and get to it.

The most powerful weapon on earth is the human soul on fire.

Ferdinand Foch

A soul on fire can warm the world.

If you want something really important to be done you must not merely satisfy the reason, you must move the heart also.

Mohandas Gandhi

Once the heart moves, everything moves.

Passion, though a bad regulator, is a powerful spring.

Ralph Waldo Emerson

You can't keep it suppressed for long!

Load up your mind with pictures capturing your preferred tomorrow. Put remembrances of the past in a place where they won't block your view.

Gary Carter

Put your past in the past.

To chop a tree quickly,
spend twice the time
sharpening the axe.

Chinese proverb

Chance favors the
prepared mind.

Louis Pasteur

**Better preparation,
better performance.**

**When you are prepared,
chance prepares to
meet you.**

Luck is what happens when preparation meets opportunity.

Richard Bach

Get prepared. Get lucky.

The more you prepare, the luckier you appear.

Terry Josephson

You can make luck happen.

No one ever achieved greatness by playing it safe.

Harry Gray

Live your life on the edge.

Plan more than you can do, then do it. Bite off more than you can chew, then chew it. Hitch your wagon to a star, keep your seat, and there you are!

Anonymous

Buckle up. Your life is taking off. Here you go!

The most effective way to do it, is to do it.

Amelia Earhart

You cannot plough a field by turning it over in your mind.

Anonymous

Any questions?

Time to get your hands dirty.

We cannot do everything at once, but we can do something at once.

Calvin Coolidge

The most important part of doctrine is the first two letters.

David Egner

Start with something.   **Make it happen. DO it!**

Don't think too much.
Do! Your intuition is
often the better guide.

Ray Bradbury

**When something feels
right, it is right for you.**

One hundred percent of
the shots you don't take
don't go in.

Wayne Gretzky

**You can't score if you
don't take a shot.**

Becoming an achiever

Scientists have proven that it's impossible to long-jump thirty feet, but I don't listen to that kind of talk. Thoughts like that have a way of sinking into your feet.

Carl Lewis

Some of the world's greatest feats were accomplished by people not smart enough to know they were impossible.

Doug Larson

Limitations are only limitations when you believe them.

One who doesn't know the limits has no limits.

When anyone tells me
I can't do anything,
I'm just not listening
any more.

Florence Griffith Joyner

**Listen to this:
You can do anything!**

What you are afraid to
do is a clear indicator of
the next thing you need
to do.

Anthony Robbins

What's next on your list?

Our doubts are traitors, and make us lose the good that we oft may win, by fearing to attempt.

William Shakespeare

Banish your doubts. Throw them out.

Whether you believe you can, or whether you believe you can't, you're absolutely right.

Henry Ford

What you believe is what you get. What are you believing?

Be a possibilitarian. No matter how dark things seem to be or actually are, raise your sights and see possibilities – always see them, for they're always there.

Norman Vincent Peale

You can often measure a person by the size of his dream.

Robert Schuller

Possibilitarians always see the light.

How big are you? S, M, L, XL, XXL?

Man is the only creature that strives to surpass himself, and yearns for the impossible.

Eric Hoffer

Beyond your very best is your even better.

The roots of true achievement lie in the will to become the best you can become.

Harold Taylor

What are you willing to become?

Nothing can stop the man with the right mental attitude from achieving his goal; nothing on earth can help the man with the wrong mental attitude.

Thomas Jefferson

There is little difference in people, but that little difference makes a big difference. That little difference is attitude. The big difference is whether it is positive or negative.

W. Clement Stone

Your attitude determines your altitude. Fly high!

Be positive. Be different.

Man is what he believes.

Anton Chekhov

Believe in who you are.

First thing every morning before you arise say out loud, 'I believe', three times.

Norman Vincent Peale

And listen as the universe says, 'We believe in you, too!'

Fortune favors the brave.

Terence McKenzie

Do more than you're supposed to do and you can have, be or do anything you want.

Bill Sands

Be bold and mighty forces will come to your aid.

What are you supposed to do? What do you want to do? What more can you do?

When I work fourteen hours a day, seven days a week, I get lucky.

Armand Hammer

Work very hard, then take a vacation.

I find that the harder I work, the more luck I seem to have.

Thomas Jefferson

Make your own luck. Work hard.

Catch on fire with enthusiasm and people will come for miles to watch you glow.

John Wesley

If a man is called to be a streetsweeper, he should sweep streets even as Michelangelo painted, or Beethoven composed music, or Shakespeare wrote poetry. He should sweep streets so well that all the hosts of heaven and earth will pause to say, here lived a great streetsweeper who did his job well.

Martin Luther King, Jr.

When you see a superstar performing, can you feel the heat? How hot are you?

Whatever you are being, be the very best.

Your limitations and success will be based on your expectations. What the mind dwells upon, the body acts upon.

Denis Waitley

Other people may not have had high expectations for me, but I had high expectations for myself.

Shannon Miller

Your body follows your mind. Take the lead.

What matters is your own expectations of you. Expect the very best.

The major reason for setting a goal is for what it makes of you to accomplish it. What it makes of you will always be of far greater value than what you get.

Jim Rohn

Worthwhile goals improve the goal setter.

There is one quality which one must possess to win, and that is definiteness of purpose, the knowledge of what one wants, and a burning desire to possess it.

Napoleon Hill

What do you want to be, do, have? Make it crystal clear.

The people who get on in this world are the people who get up and look for the circumstances they want, and, if they can't find them, make them.

George Bernard Shaw

A pessimist sees the difficulty in every opportunity; an optimist sees the opportunity in every difficulty.

Winston Churchill

Shape the world to support your dreams.

Appreciate difficulties. Embrace opportunities.

While one person hesitates because he feels inferior, another is busy making mistakes and becoming superior.

Henry Link

Put yourself in a state of mind where you say: 'Here is an opportunity for me to celebrate like never before, my own power, my ability to get myself to do whatever is necessary'.

Anthony Robbins

Those who dare, win.

Your state of mind is yours to rule. Govern with compassion, care and courage.

The real contest is always between what you've done and what you're capable of doing. You measure yourself against yourself and nobody else.

Geoffrey Gaberino

Don't measure yourself by what you have accomplished, but by what you should have accomplished with your ability.

John Wooden

Stay in the contest. Keep winning.

Do you still have a long way to go? I do.

The difference between what we do and what we are capable of doing would suffice to solve most of the world's problems.

Mohandas Gandhi

Few men during their lifetime come anywhere near exhausting the resources dwelling within them. There are deep wells of strength that are never used.

Richard Byrd

You can close the gap. You can lead the world.

Whatever you have used is just a fraction. You have so much more at your command. Use it.

People can be divided into two classes: those who go ahead and do something, and those who sit still and inquire, why wasn't it done the other way?

Oliver Wendell Holmes

To which class do you belong?

We are told that talent creates its own opportunities. But it sometimes seems that intense desire creates not only its own opportunities, but its own talents.

Eric Hoffer

Desire gives the spark. Intense desire provides the fuel.

Everyone has talent. What is rare is the courage to follow the talent to the dark place where it leads.

Erica Jong

Do not think that what your thoughts dwell upon is of no matter. Your thoughts are making you.

Bishop Steere

Trust your talents. Trust yourself. Explore!

Or breaking you. (You decide.)

We are what we think. All that we are arises with our thoughts. With our thoughts, we make our world.

Buddha

Sooner or later, those who win are those who think they can.

Richard Bach

What do *you* think?

Bingo! Jackpot! Score!

Three people were at work on a construction site. All were doing the same job, but when each was asked what the job was, the answers varied. 'Breaking rocks', the first replied. 'Earning my living', the second said. 'Helping to build a cathedral', said the third.

Peter Schultz

If I had thought about it, I wouldn't have done the experiment. The literature was full of examples that said you can't do this.

Spencer Silver

**What is your job?
What are you doing?**

Rewrite the literature.

Competing in sports has taught me that if I'm not willing to give 120 percent, somebody else will.

Ron Blomberg

Don't be afraid to give up the good to go for the great.

Kenny Rogers

The real competition starts *after* 100 percent.

If you settle for good, the great will slip away.

How would the person I want to be, do what I am about to do?

Jim Cathart

Win as if you were used to it, lose as if you enjoyed it for a change.

Eric Golnik

Know the person you aspire to be. Now, be that person.

In both, be grateful and gracious.

Most of the shadows of this life are caused by standing in one's own sunshine.

Ralph Waldo Emerson

Step aside. Let your light come shining through.

The only disability in life is a bad attitude.

Scott Hamilton

This disability is 100 percent curable. Change your attitude with dedication (not medication).

Well begun is half done.

Aristotle

Though no one can go back and make a brand new start, anyone can start from now and make a brand new ending.

Carl Bard

Plan well before you begin, and you are on your way to completion.

It's never too late to enjoy a happy childhood, adulthood or senior years. Begin yours today.

It is never too late to be what you might have been.

George Eliot

For those who believe, no proof is necessary. For those who don't believe, no proof is possible.

Harry Palmer

How young are you? 18? 28? 38? 58? 88? You are never too old to begin.

If you believe, you believe. If you don't, you don't.

A colt is worth little if it does not break its halter.

French proverb

Nothing is easier than saying words. Nothing is harder than living them day after day.

Arthur Gordon

Every great achievement is preceded by breaking the halter of prior performance. Break yours.

All know the way. Few walk it.

Strength is a matter of a made-up mind.

John Beecher

Need more strength? Make up your mind.

You have to do your own growing no matter how tall your grandfather was.

Abraham Lincoln

Make your grandfather proud. Grow up!

Make the most of yourself, for that is all there is of you.

Ralph Waldo Emerson

You are the treasure and the master of the treasure.

There comes that mysterious meeting in life when someone acknowledges who we are and what we can be, igniting the circuits of our highest potential.

Rusty Berkus

Be open to that person appearing in your life. Be that person in someone else's life.

The worst bankrupt in the world is the person who has lost his enthusiasm.

H.W. Arnold

Don't break down; keep your spirits up.

Faith is not something to grasp, it is a state to grow into.

Mohandas Gandhi

You will meet your faith along the way. And when you do, embrace it.

What you *get* by achieving your goals is not as important as what you *become* by achieving your goals.

Zig Ziglar

What are your goals? What are you becoming?

And the day came when the risk to remain tight in a bud was more painful than the risk it took to blossom.

Anaïs Nin

When your comfort zone becomes too small, break free.

People don't grow old. When people stop growing, they become old.

Grandma Moses

Change is inevitable, growth is intentional.

Glenda Cloud

Are you growing, or growing old?

**Things change.
People choose.**

If a man does not keep pace with his companions, perhaps it is because he hears a different drummer. Let him step to the music which he hears, however measured or far away.

Henry David Thoreau

Dance your own dance!

By asking for the impossible we obtain the best possible.

Giovanni Niccolini

Go ahead and ask!

Argue for your limitations and sure enough they're yours.

Richard Bach

Q: How can I set myself free?
A: Who has bound you?

Zen philosophy

Whatever you say, goes.

You are the flying bird, the cage and the door.

God wisely designed the human body so we have difficulty patting our own backs and kicking our own butts.

Jimmy Carter

Give someone else a positive pat on the back.

Learn to listen. Opportunity could be knocking at your door very softly.

Frank Tyger

Listen. Right now. Can you hear it?

Most people never run far enough on their first wind to find out if they've got a second. Give your dreams all you've got and you'll be amazed at the energy that comes out of you.

William James

Pour it on. Open throttle. Full steam ahead!

Blessed are the cracked, for they let in the light.

Omar Khan

If everyone and everything were perfect, where would be the room for improvement?

Life isn't about finding yourself. Life is about creating yourself.

George Bernard Shaw

Make your life a masterpiece.

You must take personal responsibility. You cannot change the circumstances, the seasons or the wind, but you can change yourself. That is something you have charge of.

Jim Rohn

Take life personally. Take charge.

Enlightenment means taking full responsibility for your life.

William Blake

You have within you right now everything you need to deal with whatever the world can throw at you.

Brian Tracy

Every instant, every moment, right now.

Catch it. Work with it. Throw it back!

The loftier the building, the deeper the foundation must be.

Thomas Kempis

The rung of a ladder was never meant to rest upon, but only to hold a man's foot long enough to enable him to put the other somewhat higher.

Thomas Huxley

Build your base. Work from the ground up.

Keep climbing!

In the arena of human life the honors and rewards fall to those who show their good qualities in action.

Aristotle

Concealed talent brings no reputation.

Desiderius Erasmus

**Think about it?
Talk about it?
Do it!**

Pull back the curtain and sing!

Good character is more to be praised than outstanding talent. Most talents are, to some extent, a gift. Good character, by contrast, is not given to us. We have to build it piece by piece, by thought, choice, courage, and determination.

John Adams

Good character is like a magnificent garden. All rocks carefully placed. All weeds completely pulled. Every flower in magnificent bloom.

Your talent is God's gift to you. What you do with it is your gift back to God.

Leo Buscaglia

What gifts have you received? What gifts have you given back?

Losers visualize the penalties of failure. Winners visualize the rewards of success.

Rob Gilbert

Excellence is when a woman asks of herself more than others do.

Jose Ortegay Gasset

What you see is what you will get. Which do you prefer?

Be your own boss. (A demanding one!)

Overcoming obstacles

I have missed more than 9000 shots in my career. I have lost almost 300 games. On 26 occasions I have been entrusted to take the game-winning shot and missed. I have failed over and over and over again in my life. And that is why I succeed.

Michael Jordan

I never failed once. Discovering how to make a lightbulb just happened to be a two-thousand step process.

Thomas Edison

Failure is only a stumble on the road to success.

Finding out what doesn't work is a huge step to discovering what does.

When one door closes another door opens; but we often look so long and regretfully upon the closed door that we do not see the ones which open for us.

Alexander Graham Bell

You may have a fresh start any moment you choose, for this thing that we call 'failure' is not the falling down, but the staying down.

Mary Pickford

Opportunity is knocking. Open the door.

Don't give up. Get up!

If you lose hope, somehow you lose the vitality that keeps life moving, you lose that courage to be, the quality that helps you go on in spite of it all. And so today I still have a dream.

Martin Luther King, Jr.

Don't cry when the sun is gone. Tears won't let you see the stars.

Violeta Parra

Losing hope is losing everything.

Look up! A galaxy of new joy awaits you.

If you're going through hell, keep going.

Winston Churchill

We either make ourselves miserable, or we make ourselves strong. The amount of work is the same.

Carlos Castaneda

When the going gets tough, the tough get going.

What are *you* working on?

Always look at what you have left. Never look at what you have lost.

Robert Schuller

Before my accidents, there were ten thousand things I could do. I could spend the rest of my life dwelling on the things that I had lost, but instead I chose to focus on the nine thousand I still had left.

W. Mitchell

Unless you are trying to lose weight!

Be grateful for all that you can, not bitter about what you cannot.

Don't let life discourage you; everyone who got where he is had to begin where he was.

Richard Evans

It is during our darkest moments that we must focus to see the light.

Aristotle Onassis

Where you are is the right place to be for where you want to go.

A laser beam cuts through steel.

When it is dark enough, you can see the stars.

Charles Beard

When fate hands us a lemon, let's try to make lemonade.

Dale Carnegie

Let a difficulty remind you of your blessings.

Look at what you've got and make the best of it.

What does not destroy me makes me strong.

Friedrich Nietzsche

If you will call your troubles experiences, and remember that every experience develops some latent force within you, you will grow vigorous and happy, however adverse your circumstances may seem to be.

John Miller

**Overcome a difficulty.
Solve a problem.
Surmount an obstacle.
Accumulate your power.**

Appreciate your troubles and your life will change forever.

The greatness comes not when things go always good for you. But the greatness comes when you're really tested, when you take some knocks, some disappointments, when sadness comes. Because only if you've been in the deepest valley can you ever know how magnificent it is to be on the highest mountain.

Richard Nixon

The darkest moments of life prepare us for the brightest.

I became an optimist when I discovered that I wasn't going to win any more games by being anything else.

Earl Weaver

**Be an optimist.
Be a winner.**

It's hard to beat a person who never gives up.

Babe Ruth

You can be unbeatable.

The best years of your life are the ones in which you decide your problems are your own. You do not blame them on your mother, the ecology or the president. You realize that you control your own destiny.

Albert Ellis

Make the rest of your life the best of your life.

If you want to conquer fear, don't sit at home and think about it. Go out and get busy.

Dale Carnegie

Action can melt all fears.

What counts is not necessarily the size of the dog in the fight. It's the size of the fight in the dog.

Dwight Eisenhower

What's the size of the fight in you?

Patience and perseverance have a magical effect before which difficulties disappear and obstacles vanish.

John Adams

Many of life's failures are people who did not realize how close they were to success when they gave up.

Thomas Edison

Keep going and you will prevail.

Give up the thought of giving up. There's a light bulb around the corner.

Most of the important things in the world have been accomplished by people who have kept on trying when there seemed to be no hope at all.

Dale Carnegie

When I hear somebody sigh, 'Life is hard', I am always tempted to ask, 'Compared to what?'

Sydney Harris

No hope? No way. Keep trying.

Love your life now. You can explore the alternatives later.

What happens is not as important as how you react to what happens.

Thaddeus Golas

Kites rise highest against the wind, not with it.

Winston Churchill

Sit back or bounce back. You decide.

In your struggles are the seeds of great achievement.

People are like stained-glass windows. They sparkle and shine when the sun is out, but when the darkness sets in, their true beauty is revealed only if there is a light from within.

Elisabeth Kübler-Ross

It takes twenty years to become an overnight success.

Eddie Cantor

Nurture the light within yourself. Admire the light in others.

Overnight success happens over time.

When life appears a daily grind with people and things that annoy, do something pleasant for someone else and your world will light up with joy.

Ron Kaufman

Say something nice to the next person you meet. Watch what happens – and enjoy it.

When I look back on all these worries, I remember the old man on his deathbed who said, 'I've had a lot of trouble in my life, most of which never happened'.

Winston Churchill

Worrying is like scurrying. It takes lots of energy, but gets you nowhere.

Our greatest glory is not in never failing, but in rising up every time we fail.

Ralph Waldo Emerson

The only real failure is not to try again.

If opportunity doesn't knock, build a door.

Milton Berle

Opportunities come to those who seek them.

Behind every successful person there's a lot of unsuccessful years.

Bob Brown

If you are right all the time, what's the point of going to school?

Brighten Kaufman

Appreciate the hard times behind you.

What a gift it is to live and learn and grow.

Freedom is what you do with what's been done to you.

Jean-Paul Sartre

After what's been done, you can be a chooser: to be a winner or a loser.

Better to light a candle than to curse the darkness.

Chinese proverb

Step into the light.

In any moment of decision the best thing you can do is the right thing, the next best thing is the wrong thing, and the worst thing you can do is nothing.

Theodore Roosevelt

The secret of success is constancy of purpose.

Benjamin Disraeli

Do something!

Find your purpose – and live it.

It takes courage to make a fool of yourself.

Charlie Chaplin

Patience is the companion of wisdom.

Augustine of Hippo

Imagine all those who tried to fly before Wilbur and Orville Wright succeeded. They were considered fools by many. But they were right: humans can fly.

Which virtues are your companions?

4

Living life fully

The minute you choose to do what you really want to do, it's a different kind of life.

R. Buckminster Fuller

A life worth living.

Look at everything as though you were seeing it either for the first or last time. Then your time on earth will be filled with glory.

Betty Smith

Relish every moment.

All we need to make us happy is something to be enthusiastic about.

Charles Kingsley

Choose to enthuse!

Life is a great big canvas, and you should throw all the paint you can on it.

Danny Kaye

Make a splash!

Let's make this dance upon the Earth the best that it can be. It's up to us together now. Life responds to you and me.

Ron Kaufman

Move joyfully with the rhythm of life.

I want to be scared. I want to feel unsure. That's the only way I learn, the only way I feel challenged.

Connie Chung

Outside your comfort zone is much more life waiting to be lived.

Finish each day and be done with it. You have done what you could. Some blunders and absurdities no doubt crept in; forget them as soon as you can. Tomorrow is a new day; begin it well and serenely and with too high a spirit to be encumbered with your old nonsense.

Ralph Waldo Emerson

Everything can be taken from a man or a woman but one thing: the last of human freedoms – to choose one's attitude in any given set of circumstances, to choose one's own way.

Victor Frankl

Every day is a brand new day. No nonsense!

No one can decide your attitude. Only you can do that for yourself.

I cannot always control
what goes on outside.
But I can always control
what goes on inside.

Wayne Dyer

You can complain
because roses have
thorns, or you can
rejoice because thorns
have roses.

Zig Ziglar

The outer world belongs to all. The inner world is yours alone.

Complain or rejoice. It's always your choice.

If you don't change your beliefs, your life will be like this forever. Is that good news?

Robert Anthony

What do you believe about yourself?

Accept the challenges so that you can feel the exhilaration of victory.

George Patton

No challenge, no victory. How boring!

It is not because things are difficult that we do not dare; it is because we do not dare that things are difficult.

Seneca

A happy person is not a person in a certain set of circumstances, but rather a person with a certain set of attitudes.

Hugh Downs

If you can feel the dare, rise to the challenge.

Which attitudes make *you* happy?

I can't change the direction of the wind, but I can adjust my sails to always reach my destination.

James Dean

Don't say you don't have enough time. You have exactly the same number of hours per day that were given to Helen Keller, Louis Pasteur, Michelangelo, Mother Teresa, Leonardo da Vinci, Thomas Jefferson and Albert Einstein.

Jackson Brown

A good skipper makes love with the wind.

24/7/365 is your time to be awake and alive.

The secret of your future is hidden in your daily routine.

Mike Murdock

He who is not busy being born is busy dying.

Bob Dylan

If all your days are like today, what will be your future?

Are you growing old, or old and growing?

If you view all the things that happen to you, both good and bad, as opportunities, then you operate out of a higher level of consciousness.

Les Brown

Everything in your life is an opportunity.

Do you know what my favorite part of the game is? The opportunity to play.

Mike Singletary

Life itself is a game. Play full out!

I want to sing like the birds sing, not worrying about who hears or what they think.

Rumi

Yesterday's the past and tomorrow's the future. Today is a gift. That's why we call it the present.

Spencer Johnson

What gives you great pleasure? Enjoy it.

Sign in a casino: 'You must be present to win.'

You can't have a better tomorrow if you are thinking about yesterday all the time.

Charles Kettering

I try to learn from the past, but I plan for the future by focusing exclusively on the present. That's where the fun is.

Donald Trump

You don't read a book backwards. Turn the page.

Have fun – right now.

Yesterday is a cancelled check: forget it. Tomorrow is a promissory note: don't count on it. Today is ready cash: use it!

Edwin Bliss

Cash in on a great day.

Our task is not to fix blame for the past, but to fix a course for the future.

John F. Kennedy

Set sail for your most beautiful horizon.

Live your imagination, not your history.

Stephen Covey

When I am anxious it is because I am living in the future. When I am depressed it is because I am living in the past.

Shakti Gawain

Don't just copy the old masters. Paint your own magnificent picture.

Live your life in the present.

I've got a great ambition to die of exhaustion rather than boredom.

Angus Grossart

If, before going to bed every night, you will tear a page from the calendar and remark, 'There goes another day of my life, never to return', you will become time conscious.

Zu Tavern

What will you be? All used up, or bored to death?

Don't waste your time.

Every morning you are handed twenty-four golden hours. They are one of the few things in this world you get free of charge. If you had all the money in the world, you couldn't buy an extra hour. What will you do with this priceless treasure?

Anonymous

Things turn out best for people who make the best of the way things turn out.

John Wooden

Use it or lose it.

Attitude is everything.

Let us endeavor to live that when we come to die even the undertaker will be sorry.

Mark Twain

The meaning of things lies not in the things themselves, but in our attitude towards them.

Antoine de Saint-Exupéry

It's your life. Give it all you've got.

The moon is a symbol of dark brooding, and of delicious romance.

Our attitude toward life determines life's attitude towards us.

Earl Nightingale

Life is ten percent what you make it and ninety percent how you take it.

Irving Berlin

What goes around, comes around.

One hundred percent is in your hands. Take it the way you like!

In good times, prepare for bad times. In bad times remember the good times.

Ron Kaufman

Anyone who says sunshine brings happiness has never danced in the rain.

Joyce Perz

Life is always conspiring to do better things for you than you can possibly imagine for yourself.

Don't be afraid to get your feet wet.

A man is not old until
regrets take the place
of dreams.

John Barrymore

Dream on!

Always do your best.
What you plant now,
you will harvest later.

Og Mandino

**A foundation is required
for you to reach the sky.**

That's the thing about faith. If you don't have it, you can't understand it. And if you do, no explanation is necessary.

Kira Nerys

Faith is like electricity. You can't see it, but you can see the light.

Anonymous

No explanation required. Understand?

Faith is invisible, powerful and available.

To speak gratitude is courteous and pleasant, to enact gratitude is generous and noble, but to live gratitude is to touch Heaven.

Johannes Gaertner

Someone's sitting in the shade today because someone planted a tree a long time ago.

Warren Buffett

Be grateful for Heaven on Earth.

Have you planted many trees? Will you?

Someone once asked me, 'Why do you always insist on taking the hard road?' I replied, 'Why do you assume I see two roads?'

Anonymous

Wherever you go, go with all your heart.

Confucius

The path you see is the right path.

Bon voyage!

Do not dwell in the past, do not dwell in the future, concentrate your mind on the present moment.

Buddha

Take a chance! All life is a chance. The person who goes the furthest is generally the one who is willing to do and dare. The 'sure thing' boat never gets far from shore.

Dale Carnegie

Be here now.

Take a chance. Go ahead – I dare you.

Accept that all of us can be hurt, that all of us can fail. I think we should follow a simple rule: 'If you can take the worst, take the risk'.

Joyce Brothers

The way I see it, if you want the rainbow, you gotta be willing to put up with the rain.

Dolly Parton

The real risk is not taking any risk.

Be ready to pay a price for the prize.

What gives light must endure burning.

Viktor Frankl

He who hesitates is last.

Mae West

May the light within you burn brightly.

Life doesn't wait.

Immense power is acquired by assuring yourself in your secret reveries that you were born to control affairs.

Andrew Carnegie

Every thought we think is creating our future.

Louise Hay

Will you take control?

Think carefully.

You will never find time for anything. If you want time you must make it.

Charles Buxton

Know the true value of time: snatch, seize and enjoy every moment.

Lord Chesterfield

Make an appointment to do what you really want.

Excuse me, have you got the time?

Thank you for choosing, reading and sharing this book. With 512 positive quotes, notes and anecdotes, this one is my favorite:

> Anyone who says sunshine brings happiness has never danced in the rain.
> – Joyce Perz

Which is your favorite quote? Who can you share it with today – a shower of sweet sunshine, a refreshing rinse of rain?

Wishing you a life of great dancing!

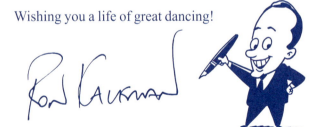

To order more copies of the **Lift Me Up!**® books, visit your local bookstore or www.LiftMeUpBooks.com